SLOUGH
A Pictorial History

Aerial photograph of the centre of Slough, *c*.1933. The road running diagonally across the photograph from top left to bottom right is the Bath Road which becomes the High Street. The church to the right of the road is St Ethelbert's Roman Catholic Church, alongside a now vanished Curzon Street. Today the church has become a landmark close to the new William Street roundabout.

SLOUGH
A Pictorial History

Judith Hunter
and
Isobel Thompson

Phillimore

1991

Published by
PHILLIMORE & CO. LTD.
Shopwyke Hall, Chichester, Sussex

ISBN 0 85033 777 1

Printed and bound in Great Britain by
BIDDLES LTD.
Guildford, Surrey

In memory of Ralph Denington
for all his help and encouragement
and his unswerving belief that Slough has a history

List of Illustrations

Frontispiece: Aerial photograph of central Slough, *c*.1933

Acknowledgements

This book could not have been compiled without the help given over many years by a great number of people. Neither of us is native to Slough, nor in our own rights do we own a collection of photographs of old Slough. Our first-hand knowledge is of the modern town, but through the many members of local history classes, friends of the museum and older residents we have built a store of knowledge which has helped us choose the photographs and write captions which will, we hope, invoke memories and trigger interest in Slough's past.

First we should like to thank the members of the Middle Thames Archaeological and Historical Society and the W.E.A. who were instrumental in setting Judith on her career as a local historian, and who campaigned for many years for a museum in Slough. We also extend our thanks to that great body of people, students, friends, colleagues, visitors and local residents, who, by their questions, research, memories and information, have helped us discover the history of Slough; our special thanks go to Kathleen Marshall and Marion Scarr for their research and untiring work at the museum and for proof reading the typescripts.

We should also like to thank Slough Councillors and officers at the Town Hall who have actively supported the museum, together with the museum Trustees for giving us the freedom to use so much of the museum's photographic archive in this book. Our special thanks also to Hitesh Ambasena, lecturer in photography at Langley College, his assistant, Chris Carter, and his predecessor, Mike Sibthorp, without whose generous help the photographic collection could not have been built up. Last, but certainly not least, we should like to thank all those who have contributed to the collection or loaned photographs specially for this book.

We have made every effort to establish copyright where possible and obtain permission to reproduce, but if we have inadvertently omitted to do so for any particular photograph we offer our sincere apologies. Our thanks to the following institutions and individuals: Aerofilms Ltd; Mr. Anstee; Mary Aylward; Peter Ballinger; Martin Barrett; Michael Bayley; Mrs. P. Beckett; Dorothy Blackman; Doris Blunden; Buckinghamshire Record Office; Mr. P. Carpenter; Mr. P. Carr; Mr. H. Clayton; Mrs. L. Garlick; Ray and Russell Grant; The Greville Organisation Ltd.; Lilian Harbard; Mr. R. Harrison; Mr. D. Isaacs; Mr. N. Jackaman; Marie Jones; Gordon Kearvell; the Lidstone family; Logan Studios; Maidenhead Library; Kathleen Marshall; Museum of English Rural Life; Mrs. L. Noriss; Post Office Archives; Rector and Wardens of Upton cum Chalvey; R.A.F. Museum, Hendon; Marion Scarr; Colin Shepherdson; Mr. G. Sherriff; Mike Sibthorp; Lydia Simmons; Mr. D. Simpson; Mr. I. Slater; Slough Borough Council; Slough Estates Ltd.; *Slough Observer*; Mrs. Taylor; Mr. A. Waring; Mr. S. Wesseley; *Windsor, Slough & Eton Express*.

Copyright remains with the owners.

Historical Introduction

To many of its residents and those who speed past the town on the M4, it comes as quite a surprise that Slough is not merely a brash modern development, but a town with a long history. Its present-day suburbs of Upton, Chalvey, Cippenham and Langley began as Saxon villages more than a thousand years ago and are as ancient as most English towns and villages. Although Slough itself is not quite so old, it came into being sometime in the century after the Norman Conquest, some eight hundred years ago. It began as a small settlement at a crossroads on the highway that linked London to Bristol, the most important medieval port outside London. Today this highway has become the A4, but for centuries it was known as the Bristol Road, and many new towns and villages grew up along its length. Later it became the Bath Road, an important coaching route, and eventually a short stretch of it became Slough High Street. The history of the road runs like a thread through the history of Slough.

The meaning of the town name is self explanatory – a slough or muddy area – but the site of the original settlement lay on a well-drained river terrace. However, only a quarter of a mile south of the crossroads, the land dropped down to the Thames flood plain. Saxon place names (such as Chalvey, which means 'calves island') tell us that land here was once quite marshy and for centuries there was a belt of marsh at the foot of the terrace. Field names such as Marsh Mead, Further Rushie Mead and Farther Marsh are found on several maps and documents, and local residents nicknamed the western part of the quagmire the 'Chalvey treacle mines'!

The road linking Windsor Castle and the new town of Windsor with the Bristol Road had to cross this belt of wet terrain. Almost impassable in winter, the nature of this treacherous, intractable mud would have been quite sufficient to cause travellers to remember the new settlement at the crossroads by its proximity to that dreadful 'slough'. The earliest surviving reference can be found in the Pipe Roll of Richard I of 1196 which records the fine of 6s. 8d. (34p) imposed on a man named Hemming de Slo (Hemming of Slough) because a villager in his tithing, named Walter Blundus, had run away from the manor.

Slough was not a manor, but lay at the junction of three – Stoke Poges, Upton and Chalvey. Both Upton and Stoke Poges are mentioned in Domesday Book and Upton has an 11th-century church, much restored, but still with several Norman features. In 1156 Upton manor and the church were given to Merton Priory in Surrey. The prior was responsible for the new chancel which was added in about 1160 and for providing the parish with its first vicar. Although the prior was Lord of the Manor and held courts in Upton, there is no evidence of any monks permanently residing there. A manor house, however, was built close to the church; the present building known as Upton Court is over six hundred years old, and is one of the oldest manor houses in Berkshire. We do not know who lived there during the Middle Ages, but at the dissolution of the monasteries it was occupied by Roger Urlwyn, rent collector for Merton Priory. In the mid-14th century there was a dispute over two cottages in Slough. Ownership was claimed by the Lord of the Manor of Chalvey, but it was the prior, Lord of the Manor of Upton, who had successfully claimed the rents.

Slough had no church of its own, not even a wayside chapel. Throughout the Middle Ages it was merely a small unimportant roadside hamlet, partly in the parish of Upton and partly in that of Stoke Poges, the boundary between them running along the centre of two of the roads which formed the crossroads. However, the Bristol Road was one of the five great medieval highways and there can have been few days in the year, winter or summer, when it was not in use. Pilgrims and pedlars, merchants and messengers and travellers of all kinds, from the king and his household to his most humble subjects, passed through Slough. It is perhaps not too fanciful to assume that from its earliest beginnings some of its inhabitants catered for these travellers, brewing ale and setting out their alestakes to announce that there were refreshments for sale.

In the 1440s Slough took on a new importance when, for about a decade, it became the site of the new brickworks for Eton College. The College was one of the earliest buildings to use the new building material introduced from the Continent. The nearest source of suitable clay was the brickearth, wind-blown material, which covered much of the river terrace on which Slough lay. In 1442 land was leased at Slough where the clay could be dug and a brick kiln was set up by order of Henry VI. Over the next nine years nearly two and a half million bricks were produced and carried by cart to Eton.

The Tudor period brought many changes. As a result of the dissolution of the monasteries by Henry VIII, Merton Priory was taken into the king's hands, and in a survey of the manor made for the Crown in 1605 we gain our first real glimpse of Slough. Thomas Duck, who lived at Upton Court, also leased Slough Farm. Its farmstead lay right in the centre of the village, more or less on the site of the old library and the present Day Centre in William Street. It was not a large farm, but its sixty or so acres lay scattered in the common fields of both Chalvey and Upton. The survey also listed the number of trees on the royal estate which were suitable for use as timber or firewood; Slough Farm had 260, and these Thomas could use for fuel and for repairing the farmhouse and buildings; mending the plough, farm carts and hedges.

The survey also includes a perambulation of the parish boundaries and the names of commons and other features long since forgotten, such as Mundaies Green near Upton Lea and Titsworth Common which lay along the Bath Road near the Tetsworth watersplash. But at Slough the only feature thought worth mentioning was the 'greate Elme' in the middle of the village. Already, however, Slough was beginning to develop its role as a thoroughfare village. The Bristol Road had become one of the five post roads, with Maidenhead the nearest postal town. Its traffic had increased many fold and by 1577 Slough had three alehouses. In contrast there were only two in the rest of the parish, though the neighbouring thoroughfare town of Colnbrook had at least eight, as well as ten inns. Waggons had begun to replace pack horses and the road was one of the main routes for wool and cloth destined for the London cloth market.

Slough, however, was a hamlet and far less important than either Colnbrook or Maidenhead, two small towns which had been elevated to boroughs by royal charter during the 16th century. It could not boast of even one inn. The first reference to inns at Slough is found in the account books of Sir Giles Mompesson, the wily M.P. who, in 1617, obtained a grant from the Crown to license inns throughout the country. A year later he licensed the *Crown* and the *Reindeer* in Slough. By the time the first stage coach rumbled its way through Slough to Bristol in 1657, Slough had at least two more – the

White Hart and the *Red Lion* – and was on the way to becoming an important stage on the road. The Bristol Road was renamed the Bath Road when Bath became the great pleasure resort, a mecca for the nobility and pleasure seekers of all strata of society. In 1711 Thomas Baldwin, landlord of the *Crown*, advertised a new stage coach service from London to Bath. By 1718 his thrice-weekly service had been extended and the first daily service established. Soon after this the Colnbrook Turnpike Trust was founded and for a few years there was a toll gate to the west of Slough. The efforts of the Trust to improve the state of the Bath Road were not very effective, but stones and gravel were carted to fill the pot holes. The road was widened at Salt Hill and other places, and flat bridges were built over the streams which crossed the road. The turnpike trustees held their meetings at various inns, including the *Crown* at Slough, and the *Windmill* and *Castle* at Salt Hill.

Slough was now an important thoroughfare village, sharing with Colnbrook the role of the second stage from London. It had some thirty or so houses, including at least seven inns and alehouses – the *Crown, Reindeer, Red Lion, White Hart, Bear, Black Boy* and the *Pied Horse*. By the 1740s, however, it had another rival, Salt Hill, a small roadside village a mile to the west of Slough. Daniel Defoe, author of *A Journey through England and Wales*, commented on the competition of the new inns at Salt Hill in the second edition of his book. The *Windmill* and *Castle* inns were prestigious establishments catering for the stage coaches and the more high class posting trade. Slough, however, held its own, and while Salt Hill kept the cream of the post horse business, the stage coach and waggon trade was concentrated in Slough. By the end of the 18th century its houses had begun to spread along the Bath Road towards Langley and a new coaching inn, the *Dolphin*, was built at the Langley Road junction. Slough also now had a coachmaker, wheelwright, farrier and several other small businesses, including Thomas Brown's nursery. Its population had now reached about two hundred.

Its most important inhabitant was William Herschel who had come to Slough in 1786. Five years earlier he had discovered the planet Uranus, an event which had roused such great scientific interest that George III appointed him his own private astronomer. In order to take up this appointment, Herschel left Bath, where he had been an organist, to live near Windsor. Eventually, after two moves, he set up home with his sister, Caroline, at Slough in a house in Windsor Road which became known as Observatory House. Here he cut down all the trees and installed his 20-foot telescope, and began work on his giant 40-foot instrument. Herschel and his telescopes literally put Slough 'on the map', for not only did they make Slough famous, but when the first Ordnance Survey map of the area was published in 1822, the site of the 40-foot telescope was clearly marked.

At the end of the 18th century South Buckinghamshire was predominantly a rural area and the countryside around Slough still had many of its ancient commons and greens and remnants of its common open fields, each divided into numerous unhedged strips. Slough Farm was still in the centre of the village and Chalvey Manor Farm, Upton Lea Farm, Upton Court Farm and Plough Leys were all to be found within a mile. But here, as in so many other parts of the country, the agricultural scene was changing. The old ways were regarded as unprogressive, inhibitive to the use of new machinery, improved crops and livestock. There was pressure and incentive to enclose the commons and common fields and redistribute the old strips to make larger compact fields, each under single ownership. One by one Inclosure Acts were passed for many of the South Buckinghamshire parishes, releasing land from the restrictions of common grazing rights and giving those landowners and farmers who could afford it opportunity to revolutionise their farming. Miles of new hedges were planted and commons such as Chalvey Green disappeared. New crops were grown, but the removal of the grazing rights from over two thousand acres in the area of modern Slough also opened up the possibilities for other uses for the land.

The Upton cum Chalvey Inclosure Act was passed in 1810, but it was not until the 1820s that we find the first hint of change. By this date Upton Church was in a very poor condition and rather than expend money to repair and enlarge it, the decision was made to build a new one near Slough. The reason given in the correspondence was the rise of the population since the Inclosure Act. An educational survey of 1816/18 gives a total population of about 500 for the two villages of Slough and Upton. The other village in the parish of Upton cum Chalvey had a population of just over 400. Land which had once been farmland was being developed for houses and shops. In 1823, 21 shops and small businesses were advertised in the local trade directory. St Mary's Church (though it did not yet have this name) was opened in 1836, a mean building which favoured neither the prosperous inhabitants of the parish nor its poorer members. The same year the Union Workhouse was opened to serve the 19 parishes of South Buckinghamshire; it was built near the church in that no man's area between Upton and Slough. Such workhouses were the outcome of the Poor Law Amendment Act of 1834, a measure to reduce the rates rather than help the poor and needy. Even so, it became the old people's home, orphanage, home for unmarried mothers, lunatic asylum and doss house for some two hundred and more unfortunate men, women and children who had become destitute. It was an unpleasant place, and meant to be so, but this workhouse in Slough was not as bad as some others. It had a school and infirmary and there are hints in the records of some kindliness; the one cruel master was quickly dismissed.

In 1836, when the church and workhouse were built, Slough was still an important coaching village. More than thirty coaches sped through daily in both directions, to such far flung places as London, Bristol, Bath, Birmingham, Oxford, Gloucester and Worcester. Several of them changed horses in Slough at the *Crown*, *Red Lion*, *White Hart*, or the *Dolphin*. The *White Hart* was also a receiving house for the mail which came by foot postman from Colnbrook. The *Crown* was still the most important inn and had a substantial trade providing postchaise and post horses for those who could afford such means of transport. The village could now boast many more shops and businesses including two bakers, three shoemakers, two carpenters, a chair manufactory, a chemist, coachmaker, a coal and corn dealer, four grocery shops, a milliner, plumbers, Brown's Nursery, a saddler, two tailors and a surgeon. Clearly it was a busy village, far outstripping Upton and Chalvey and other neighbouring villages in the facilities it provided. Slough also had two private schools, but the only ones providing an education for the poorer members of the community were at Upton and Chalvey.

Nationally the 19th century was one of unprecedented population growth, the population doubling during the first fifty years. In South Buckinghamshire, growth was at first relatively slow; it was a rural area and urban areas were growing at the expense of the rural. Some parishes even suffered a drop in numbers in the middle years of the century as families left the countryside to work in the towns. In contrast, the population of Upton cum Chalvey, and Slough in particular, rose steeply. The 1830s growth is partly accounted for by the influx of inmates to the workhouse, but in 1835 work began on the Great Western Railway from London to Bristol. It was soon to provide an incentive for growth and within a decade Slough had been transformed from a village to a small market town. The 1851 census records 357 houses, 103 shops and small businesses and a population of just over 1,500. The rest of the parish contained 289 houses with a total population of 3,573.

Not all welcomed the coming of the railway. In 1834 a protest meeting at the *Windmill Inn* attracted a good crowd, though only a year later, when the Railway Act received the royal assent, the same inn was used for a celebratory dinner. Of the people who opposed the railway, it was the Provost and Fellows of Eton College who had the most influence. Fearing that the accessibility of a fast means of transport to London would be very bad for school discipline, they successfully persuaded Parliament to insert a clause in the Act prohibiting any railway station being built within three miles of the College. Thus no station was planned for Slough. Instead a station was built at Langley, a convenient location even for those who wished to use it as a terminus to Windsor. Windsor was not yet served by a railway, but two turnpike roads led there from the Bath Road – one from Slough through Eton to Windsor Bridge, the other from Langley Broom through Datchet to the old Datchet Bridge.

Three months before the railway opened in June 1838, the minute books of the railway directors record the duties of the Langley stationmaster – and yet when the trains began running this station remained closed. Instead the trains stopped at Slough, without the benefit of either platform or station. Tickets were at first sold at the *Crown Inn* and then at the newly opened *North Star Tavern* with its purpose-built ticket office. Surviving records do not name the person responsible for the change of plans, but circumstantial evidence points to William Bonsey Esq., of Belle Vue House, and the owner of Slough Farm. If this had not happened, Slough might today be a mere suburb of Langley.

The opening of a railway station, however, does not create a town. The new town of Slough was built, not at the direction of one landowner or industrialist, but by numerous people of moderate means. There was a snowball effect: it was suddenly a good place to set up business and to look for work, an attractive place to build houses or set up home. Contemporary advertisements described Slough as a 'thriving' town with 'many handsome shops and some respectable inns, the residences of many genteel and respectable families'.

By 1851 Slough had a population of some one and a half thousand, almost three hundred and fifty houses and several new streets. There was a weekly market and nearly one hundred and fifty shops and businesses, amongst them that of James Elliman, the linen draper who was already manufacturing his embrocation. Within a few years Elliman's Embrocation was to become a product of national fame. There was a Mechanics' Institute in Church Street, and a post office in the High Street, the letters now arriving by train; Colnbrook had been demoted to a sub-office. There was a Methodist church and a Congregationalist meeting place and a new National School at Arbour Vale. In 1846 Slough was chosen as the site of the first police station and lock-up to serve the Stoke Hundred; William Burke was the Police Superintendent. Petty Sessions began to be held in Slough in 1850 and within a short time its police courts were held weekly, while those at the older centres were only fortnightly or even monthly.

The railway had killed most of the long distance coaching and carrying trade, but not the inns at Slough, unlike the *Castle Inn* at Salt Hill which had closed in 1840. Those at Slough were adapted to the changing conditions. In 1853 cabs and flys were advertised for hire from five inns and public houses, and an omnibus connected Slough with Windsor. A magnificent hotel was built by the Great Western Railway Company to cater for its most noble travellers. It was appropriately named the *Royal Hotel*, for here Queen Victoria had her own waiting room. In 1849, when Windsor at last got its own railway stations, the *Royal Hotel* was doomed. It was closed in 1853, but it no longer mattered to Slough which had already become one of the largest towns in the county and the 'metropolis' of the Stoke Union.

While most of what was new was little different from that which might be found in any small market town, two industries – brickmaking and horticulture – were of wider importance. Brickmaking had probably been an intermittent industry for a long time and most of the warm red and dark bricks which characterise the early buildings were made locally. However, after the Inclosure Acts the scale of the workings began to change. The earliest known of these new brickworks was at Upton Lea; it was owned by William Fleetwood Nash, but by 1826 George Hoskins was making bricks in Slough itself. His kiln was just behind the *White Hart*. These works mark the beginning of a brickmaking industry which was to last one hundred years. In the 1850s and '60s Richard Dodd, William Liddiard and Richard Little all had brickfields or centres of operation in Slough. For many years the public house now known as the *Printers' Devil* was called the *Brickmakers Arms*, and stood adjacent to the field exploited for its brickearths by Richard Little.

No doubt, as Slough continued to grow, many of the bricks were used locally, but bricks from Slough and Langley were also sent by rail to London. In 1882 the Slough Arm of the Grand Union Canal provided a cheaper means of transport, with a double benefit. On the return trip the barges brought refuse out of the capital, some of which was used to fill the pits while the combustible material was used as fuel for the kilns. When Bedfordshire machine-made bricks threatened the industry in the early years of this century, it was this source of cheap fuel which allowed the Slough and Langley Brick Company to survive into the 1930s.

Today, it is difficult to visualise the awful noise and dust of the brickfields with their pug mills and acrid, pungent smells, but the impact of the industry on the landscape can still be seen in many streets. Wherever the brickearths were removed the land is now much lower and in streets such as Stoke Road the houses and gardens are some four feet below the level of the road.

Slough's fame in the world of horticulture also began in the 19th century. In 1837 Charles Brown introduced a new lily from China, but it was Charles Turner's Royal Nursery that was responsible for the commercial exploitation of the apple bred by Richard Cox of Colnbrook. The Cox's Orange Pippin still sells well and so does another of Turner's 'finds' – Mrs Simpkin's Pink which was named after the matron of the Union Workhouse in the 1880s. About this time the Chelsea firm, Veitch & Sons, opened nurseries in Langley and raised an apple called Langley Pippin. Their nursery ground north of the railway gave the railway traveller a beautiful view to contrast with the ugly spoil heaps and pits of the brickfields. If the acres of flowers and fruit trees have long since disappeared, Slough still has some claim to horticultural pride in as much as the Borough Parks Department frequently wins gold medals for its floral exhibits at national shows.

Slough's rate of growth continued unchecked during the second half of the 19th century, its streets and houses reaching out towards Upton and Chalvey. There were several new churches and chapels and new amenities, notably the gas company in Chandos Street, established in 1850, and the private water company in Herschel Street which in 1870 began to provide water for those who could afford to pay for it. A volunteer fire brigade was formed in 1873 and a public hall was erected in 1887. Taking advantage of the first Public Health Act, the Slough Sanitary Authority was formed in 1863. Efforts were made to tackle the problem of sewage and drainage, but with little real success until the opening of the pumping station in Chalvey in the 1880s and the purchase of Dorney Manor Farm to treat the sewage. In 1894 the Civil Parishes Act brought into being Slough Urban District. The new authority became responsible for the town of Slough and its suburb of Upton, but not Chalvey or Upton Lea. They became the civil parish of Upton cum Chalvey and part of the Eton Rural District.

By the early 20th century the town had become more industrialised with the opening of several factories, but the establishment of a Mechanical Transport Repair Depot in what had been the cornfields of Cippenham Court Farm during the last year of World War One heralded a new era of industrialisation for Slough. The depot was for the repair of war vehicles, but when hostilities ceased it was still under construction and much of the site was littered with broken vehicles. Local residents affectionately and aptly nicknamed it The Dump.

By 1919 the depot had become a monumental white elephant and the War Office was only too pleased to sell the site when a syndicate of businessmen put in a bid. The sale included not only the 600-acre site, but also the workshops, machinery and vehicles at home and abroad. The government made a handsome profit, but so did the new Slough Trading Company which before the end of the first year had sold war surplus to the value of £5,000,000. Its auctions of new and repaired cars, lorries and motor cycles brought customers from all over the country. England was now moving into the motor age and once again the Bath Road was important to the history of Slough.

By 1924 the supply of war vehicles was coming to an end and already some of the workshops were being leased to other companies. A year later new legislation authorised the company to build more roads, a power station and to lay electricity cables, water and steam mains and drains. In 1926 the company changed its name to Slough Estates Ltd. which better expressed its new role of providing factories and facilities for lease. It was the first trading estate of this kind anywhere in the world. Companies and individuals came from all over the country to set up businesses on the estate. Elsewhere in the country the late 1920s and early 1930s were years of depression, but in Slough unemployment stood at a mere one per cent. Some eight thousand people were employed on the estate, many of them from Slough and the surrounding area, but workers also came by train from London, Hounslow, Marlow and Henley; soon the estate had its own station. The possibility of work also brought people from the depressed areas of Wales and northern England. Housing became an acute problem, for although Slough Urban District Council and private developers built new houses, the supply of new homes could not keep pace with the ever increasing demand.

The Trading Estate, of course, was not actually in Slough, nor were many of the new residential areas. This changed in 1930/1 when the urban district boundaries were extended to take in considerable areas of Burnham, Farnham Royal, Stoke Poges and Langley, and the whole of Cippenham. Within a few years private and council estates covered most of the area with four new churches to serve the communities. A rather different Community Centre was built in Farnham Road to cater for the social requirements of the town's workers. In 1938 the Urban District Council opened its first proper town hall at Salt Hill – just in time to celebrate Slough's elevation to borough status.

It is now 50 years since that momentous occasion and Slough's boundaries have once again been extended to take in parts of Wexham and Britwell. New people of many kinds have come to work and live in Slough and make their mark on the townscape and enrich the life of the town. The M4 has replaced the Bath Road as the major trunk road and no longer does the traffic thunder through the High Street.

So many changes have occurred in such a short time that it becomes harder and harder to remember just what Slough used to look like even a few years back. Fortunately, Slough Museum now has an ever growing collection of photographs, a rich source for research into Slough's history and a nostalgic treasure chest.

Around the Borough

1. Slough in 1802 by John Nixon. This is the earliest known picture of Slough, and the only one showing it as a mere thoroughfare village on the Bath Road. The road had been turnpiked for over three-quarters of a century, but its rutted surface shows clearly the problems of road maintenance before John Macadam's improvements. None of the buildings shown still exist, but comparison with later photographs suggests that the view is along the High Street from east to west. The building on the right would then be the *Red Lion Inn* and beyond, past the opening into William Street, is the *White Hart*, the post office receiving house kept by Charles and Maria Luff. On the left is the *Black Boy*.

2. This is the earliest known map of Slough which shows the buildings in any detail. It was produced in 1773 when Slough was a thoroughfare village on the Bath Road with about 30 houses, seven of them inns and alehouses. The north-west quarter of the village is not shown as this was then in the parish of Stoke Poges, and the map was made for the parish of Upton cum Chalvey. As on the aerial photograph, the road running from top left to bottom right is the Bath Road/High Street.

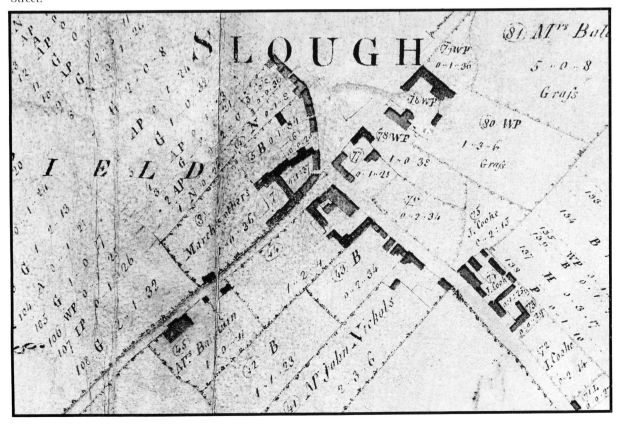

3. This view of Slough High Street taken at the turn of the century looks in the opposite direction, but towards the Crown crossroads. The *Crown Inn* stands at the junction of the High Street and Windsor Road, its 18th-century façade proclaiming its importance as a coaching inn and posting house. The tall building next door still survives. The *Red Lion* on the opposite side of the road can also be traced back to the 17th century, but it had clearly also been rebuilt. On the other hand the *Black Boy* still shows its ancient timber-framed structure; it was demolished in 1910.

4. Slough High Street looking west from the crossroads. In the middle of the photograph is the *White Hart Inn* with its distinctive Georgian façade. From about 1793 to 1841 the *White Hart* was the receiving house for letters to Slough. Notice the ornate lamp standard. When this was erected early this century there was a 20 m.p.h. speed limit through Slough. This was reduced to 10 m.p.h. in 1908 after a census was taken by the Urban District Council which showed that over 600 cars passed through the town each day. The building on the left is the *Grapes* which still survives.

5. A sketch map of the Colnbrook Penny Post route as proposed in 1813; during the trial week 99 letters were delivered to Slough. The penny referred to the charge of an extra penny for the carriage of the letters from Colnbrook to the receiving houses.

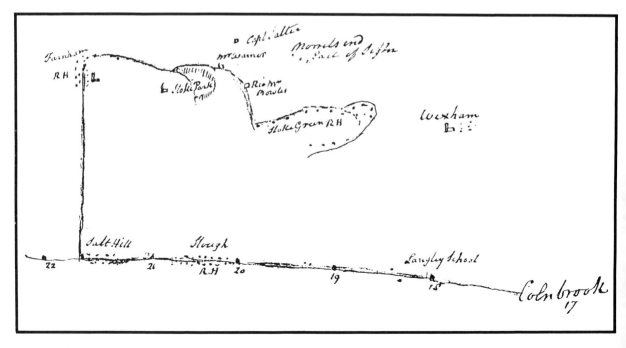

6. Slough High Street in the 1930s. A policeman stands on point duty at the crossroads, his position marked by a white circle. The old *Crown Inn* has been demolished, and its replacement stands some distance back from the pavement.

7. The north-east quarter of Crown Corner after the demolition of the *Red Lion* in 1935. Notice the advertisement for the Palace Cinema. To the left, rising above the hoardings, are the tower of St Ethelbert's Church and the roof line of 'The Cedars', the old farmhouse of Slough Farm.

8. Obverse and reverse of a halfpenny token issued by the landlord of the *Red Lion Inn* in 1794.

9. 'Cedar House' and St Ethelbert's Church, *c.*1937. 'Cedar House' was originally the homestead of Slough Farm, which occupied most of this corner of Slough until after the coming of the railway. By the end of the century the house was tenanted by Dr. Buee. It was bought by Slough Urban District Council in 1904 and some four years later it became the Urban District Offices. After its demolition, a library was built on the site. This building is now a Day Centre.

10. Crown Corner looking towards the north-east, probably in the late 1930s. A new building has replaced the old *Red Lion Inn* and the hoardings shown in plate 7.

11.-13. Slough was made a 'safety town' in 1952 and during 1956 and 1957 was the subject of a Ministry of Transport experiment. The Belisha beacon was introduced in 1950, the zebra crossing in 1952 and the light controlled crossing in 1956.

PEDESTRIAN CROSSING PROGRESS

1950, *Belisha Crossing*

1952, *Zebra Crossing*

1956, *Light Controlled Crossing*

14. Slough High Street looking west towards Crown Corner. In the far distance can be seen the *Grapes*, first licensed in 1830 within months of the passing of the Beerhouse Act. On the right the ornate lamp belongs to the *Reindeer Inn*, which dates back to the early 17th century. Notice the meat hanging outside the butcher's shop. The *Grapes* and most of the shops on the left of the picture survive, although the wrought-iron balconies have disappeared.

15. Slough High Street looking west, further along the road, *c.*1913. The *Floral Arms* and the entrance to Alpha Street can just be seen on the left and opposite are the gates to H. Bryant's photographic studio. Next to it is the *Crown and Anchor*. Notice the advertisements for stabling, cyclists and parcels.

16. The High Street looking east in the 1950s. The junction of The Grove and the High Street dominated by the Methodist Central Hall, which was opened by H.R.H. The Duchess of York (now the Queen Mother) in 1932. It was demolished in the 1960s.

17. Sussex Place, at the turn of the century. Until recently Sussex Place was an extension of the High Street, part of the old Bath Road. Its first houses were built in the 1830s, modest, elegant houses for the genteel with modest means.

18. Windsor Road looking south, *c*.1900. The part of the road nearest the camera was known as Arbor Hill. To the left is an entrance to Upton Park and Albert Street, and to the right Chalvey Road East. From Arbor Hill the Windsor Road descended steeply to Arbor Vale, from the well-drained land of the old river terrace to the marshy area of the Thames Flood Plain. Here was once the marsh that gave Slough its name.

19. This view of the Windsor Road looking north was taken in the 1890s. The *Rising Sun* is still on the same site, but like many of Slough's public houses has been rebuilt.

20. William Street looking north from Crown Corner at the turn of the century. The cow being driven along the street had probably just been bought at Slough cattle market. J. Walton took over the *Clock House* and made it into a temperance hotel in 1915. The temperance movement was an attempt by various churches, especially the Methodists, from the middle of the last century to well into this century, to fight the excessive consumption of alcohol and its attendant problems. A close neighbour of the *Red Lion Hotel* and *Crown Inn*, the *Clock House* was well placed to confront its rivals head on by offering an alternative, alcohol-free place to eat and socialise. It was demolished in 1925.

21. Stoke Road looking north, *c.*1900. In the distance is St Paul's Mission Church. On the left the *Brickmakers' Arms* (today the *Printers' Devil*), built by Mr. Little, a brickmaker who leased a field from Mr. William Bonsey. The lease was to run for seven years and covered the use of the brickearths for making bricks. Mr. Little is commemorated in the name Littledown Road built on the site of his field.

22. The Mackenzie Street and High Street junction, *c.*1900. Until the redevelopment of the centre of the town, Mackenzie Street led through to Station Approach. Most buildings in this photograph have survived.

23. Well into this century Mackenzie Street, like several other side roads, had a country look, each house still having its own front garden.

24. The Grove was first developed in the 1850s, but it was still a leafy lane some fifty years later. The house in the High Street, which can be seen in the centre of the photograph, is Turner's Nursery.

25.   Upton village centre early in the 19th century. Upton is the oldest part of Slough, a Saxon village built on the very edge of the terrace overlooking the Thames Flood Plain. St Laurence's Church is Norman, here shown with its tower covered in ivy. It was the parish church until 1836. The road in the centre of the picture is the driveway of Upton Court, a medieval manor house. On the left of the picture is Upton Road and the pound where stray animals were impounded.

26.   The *Red Cow* was opened as a beer shop in 1830 in a 16th-century building which stood on the opposite side of the road to the present *Red Cow*. It was probably given its name because Charles Mountford was a butcher, and his widow had a small dairy business. The *Red Cow* moved into the present building about 1860 when John Purser became the licensee. The drawing was made in the 1870s or 1880s sometime after the beer shop had begun selling Ashby's Entire.

27.   A picturesque view of Upton Park, drawn soon after the park was built in the 1840s by James Bedborough. The elegant houses with their own gatehouses and pleasure grounds were well sited to attract the prosperous classes who wished to be near Eton and the Court at Windsor, and the new railway station at Slough which gave easy access to London. Today the grounds are known as Herschel Park.

28. Children inspecting the new illuminated school sign in Wexham Road, Upton Lea, in 1956. Upton Lea takes its name from a farm of that name which can be traced back to the 17th century. The school itself is visible in the distance on the right of the photograph.

29.   Of all the villages which now make up Slough, Chalvey had the strongest sense of community and independence. In the early 19th century it was larger than either Slough or Upton. Now nothing remains of its busy High Street except the name.

30.   Chalvey Grove, an ancient lane which takes its name from part of the old wooded village green. It still follows the same curved line, but is now lined by houses.

31. The path to Queen Anne's Well at Chalvey from opposite the *Windmill* at Salt Hill in the 1950s. Both Queen Charlotte and Queen Anne had water brought from a spring in Chalvey to Windsor Castle and it is thought that Queen Anne had the well dug.

32. The *Three Tuns* crossroads, the centre of the small thoroughfare hamlet of Salt Hill. The *Three Tuns* was one of the smaller inns that catered for travellers along the Bath Road during the coaching era; it is still in existence in the original 18th-century building, but is not visible in this photograph. The largest and most important coaching inn was the *Windmill*, named after a windmill that stood in Windmill Field to the south of the road.

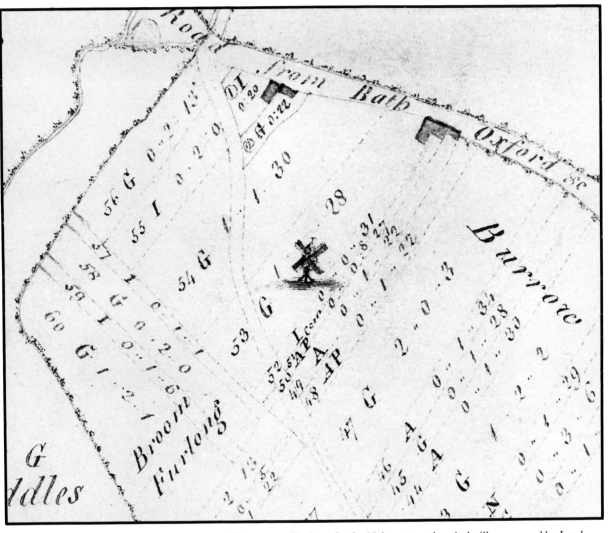

33. The windmill shown on the 1773 map of Upton cum Chalvey. In the 18th century the windmill was owned by Lord Godolphin and tenanted by Thomas Woolhouse. When the windmill was burnt down, Thomas rebuilt it, though he had difficulty in getting the money from the Godolphin family because of the untimely death of Lord Godolphin.

34. Large, desirable residences on the Bath Road at Slough. These were demolished to make way for the Town Hall extension. The house on the corner of Ledgers Road was known as High Fields; it was the home of the Jackaman family.

35. The pond at Cippenham, the centre of the old village.

36. Mill Stream Lane and the Green at Cippenham. The mill commemorated in the road name was the Ay Mill (later Hay Mill) north of Cippenham. Cippenham Green is the only village green which has survived in the area; it has been administered by a trust since the end of the 19th century.

37. Britton's tea rooms and gardens, Cippenham, in the 1920s. The era of the tea room began with the motor age.

38. An aerial photograph of the Britwell Estate before the houses were built in 1955. The estate was owned by the Greater London Council and was intended to provide homes for Londoners. The built-up area at the top right of the picture lies west of the Farnham Road, beginning with the Crofthill housing development and stretching eastwards towards Manor Park.

39. Windsor Lane, Burnham, looking north. Today the *Harvester Inn* (the old *Red Squirrel*) stands on the site of the wood in the distance. This area was part of Burnham parish until 1930.

40. One of the main road bridges crossing the railway north of the town. With a characteristic lack of foresight, almost all the railway bridges crossing the main line were only wide enough for one vehicle and were built with a distinctive, but awkward, kink. The last of these is the Leigh Road bridge in the Trading Estate.

41. Farnham Road in the mid-1930s; earlier 20th-century houses were soon to make way for new shops.

42.   A new housing estate off Stoke Poges Lane. In 1921 Carrington Road marked the boundary of Slough; beyond lay the fields of Stoke Poges. In early 1921 work had come to a standstill as the builders were unable to recruit sufficient labour. The line running diagonally across the bottom right of the photograph marks the boundary between the new estate and older houses. The land level had been lowered by the removal of brickearth, and thus the gardens of the new houses are several feet higher than those of the old. This is the site of Mr. Little's brickfield lying to the west of Stoke Road.

STOKE POGES LANE ESTATE

THE GARDEN SUBURB OF SLOUGH

SOUTH BUCKS.

Phone :
ESTATE OFFICE,
SLOUGH 1228.

**STOKE POGES HOMESTEADS LTD.,
226, HIGH STREET,
SLOUGH.**

Phone :
HIGH STREET,
SLOUGH 294.

43. A 1930s brochure for a housing estate on the west of Stoke Poges Lane. It was one of several to be described as a 'garden suburb'.

44. The Stoke Poges Lane estate office. This company had land to build 2,000 houses.

45. Interior of one of the houses. A six-room house cost £445 or a deposit of £25 and a weekly repayment of 11s. 2d.; rates and water cost 2s. 9d. per week.

46. A prize garden at 29 Loddon Spur – worthy of a 'garden suburb'.

47. Rent collectors were not always as warmly welcomed as this one photographed in 1956 in Stoke Poges Lane estate, but to have a house at all was a luxury for many in the inter-war years and the 1950s. Large numbers of houses were built by the council and private developers, but for many years building could not keep up with demand and the arrival of yet more immigrants from the depressed areas of the country and from overseas.

48. Wexham Post Office. Not all the houses in the suburbs were built this century. This timber-framed house is at least 300 years old and when first built stood on the edge of Wexham and Stoke Green. This area of Slough was only incorporated into the borough in 1974 when Slough became part of Berkshire.

49. The centre of Langley parish was, of course, St Mary's Church, but until about a hundred years ago there were few buildings near the church, only the two sets of 17th-century almshouses, the tiny vicarage next to the church wall, the girls' school and the *Red Lion*. The pub was owned by the church and had once been known as the Church House; it provided an income for repairing the fabric of the church.

50. Langley did not develop a High Street until the mid-19th century and in earlier times this part of the parish was known as Horsemoor Green.

51. Meadfield Road was laid out by the enclosure commissioners in 1813 to give access to the new smaller fields which replaced the old medieval Mead Field. It did not become a residential area until the present century.

Bath Road, Langley.

52. When the *William IV* (now renamed *King William*) was opened as a beershop in 1866, it was almost the only building in this stretch of the London Road. Until the Langley Enclosure Act this part of the road crossed a small heath known as Langley Broom which was the scene of at least two highway robberies.

53. The *Montague Arms*, Bath Road, Langley. The house is now a Harvester Inn, but in the mid-18th century it was known as the *Waggon and Horses*, a small and isolated inn on the Bath Road. Its name changed first to the *Lord Beaulieu's Arms* and then to the *Montague Arms* after the families that lived in Ditton Park. Notice the weighing machine, the horse trough and the notice over the entrance to the garden: 'Cyclists welcome, teas provided'.

54. John Cary's map of the High Roads around London, 1790. Notice the separate villages of Slough and Salt Hill and the isolated inns – the *White Horse*, *Dolphin* and the *Lord Beaulieu's Arms*. The straight lines are suggested lines of sight for the bored coach passenger being driven at 7 m.p.h. Notice the small heath near *Lord Beaulieu's Arms* known as Langley Broom. In 1722 Benjamin Child was hanged here and his body was then left on a gibbet to deter others.

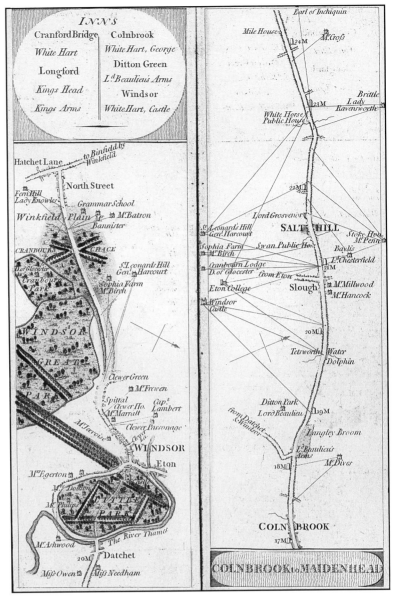

55. Brands Hill, Colnbrook. With the enlargement of Slough's boundaries in 1930/1, the urban district took in this area known as Brands Hill, which was more properly part of Colnbrook than Slough. It was little more than ribbon development along the Bath Road and in the 1920s and '30s Kelly's Cabin was a well known stopping place for cyclists.

Farms, Factories & Shops

56. Cippenham Court Farm was the largest farm in Slough in the early years of this century. It can be traced back to the 15th century and was almost certainly the demesne farm of Cippenham Manor. Just south of the farmhouse was the deer park created for Richard Earl of Cornwall (younger son of King John). The park became a farm in the 15th century and some of the surviving structures were built about 1600. It ceased to be a farm in about 1980. The farmhouse, built *c.*1820, has been converted to offices and the stables are now the *Long Barn*.

During 1909 and 1910 the Headington family, tenant farmers of Cippenham Court Farm, made a photographic survey of the farm. The surviving album shows the work of a mixed farm with sheep, dairy cows, stud and work horses, and arable fields stretching far north of the Bath Road. See plates 57-60.

57. Ploughing.

58. Threshing.

59. Sheep-shearing.

60. Lunch break.

61. Station Road looking south: a rural scene in the centre of Langley early this century. The cows belong to Place Farm which can be seen on the right of the photograph. Today the site of the farmstead has become part of Langley College complex.

62. The arrival of the Mogul 16 h.p. tractor at Cippenham Farm in 1915 was a momentous occasion; it was the first tractor in the district. The photograph was taken in a field near Everitts Corner; behind the hedge is the Bath Road.

63. Slough cattle market, c.1920-22. Cattle auctions in Slough date back to 1850. At first they were held once a month, but in 1863 they were increased to once a week. The cattle market shown in the photograph was organised by Buckland & Sons, auctioneers. It was held for many years in the centre of the town, close to William Street, and was only moved during the 1960s to make way for the new Slough College (now Thames Valley College).

SOME OF HIS MAJESTY'S SHEEP

AMONG THE PIGS

64. The king's fatstock at Slough cattle market, 1904. This picture appeared in the *Daily Graphic* on 7 December, the day after the fatstock sale at Slough. The autioneer was F. W. Buckland.

65.   Charles Turner's Nursery, with its beautiful wisteria, was a splendid site in Slough High Street for nearly a hundred years. Vividly remembered by older residents, surprisingly few photographs of it have been found. Horticulture was very important in the Slough area and Turner's Nursery was responsible for putting many well known products on the market, including the Cox's Orange Pippin, Mrs. Sinkins Pink and the Crimson Rambler Rose.

66.   Brickmaking was one of the most important industries in Slough for over a hundred years and much of Victorian London was built from bricks made in this area. This photograph, taken in the late 1920s, shows Smith's Brickfields at Langley Park Road just north of the canal. The bricks were stacked in rows to dry before being burned in the kiln. The smoke on the extreme left marks the site of the kiln. The shed in the middle right housed the engine which drove the pug (clay) grinder.

67. Langley brickfield workers posing for a photograph. The men worked in teams which included the moulder (who employed the other members of the team), temperer, off-bearer, ropers-in, walk flatter, pug boy and barrow loader.

68. The Slough Arm of the Grand Union Canal was opened in 1882. It was built to serve the brick-making industry and it had been proposed that the canal should extend much further west, but because several local landowners raised objections it had to terminate in Slough. This photograph was taken in the early years of this century. The Slough Arm is now no longer used commercially.

69. Elliman Sons & Co.'s factory. 'Elliman's Embrocation', a rub for sprained muscles well known since the late 19th century, was manufactured in the Elliman factory on Chandos Street, Slough. The factory was built after the death in 1870 of James Elliman, Snr, who started the business, by his son, James Elliman, Jnr. The embrocation was exported to countries all over the world. Today the Queensmere shopping centre stands on the site. Elliman's Embrocation can still be bought, but it is no longer produced in Slough.

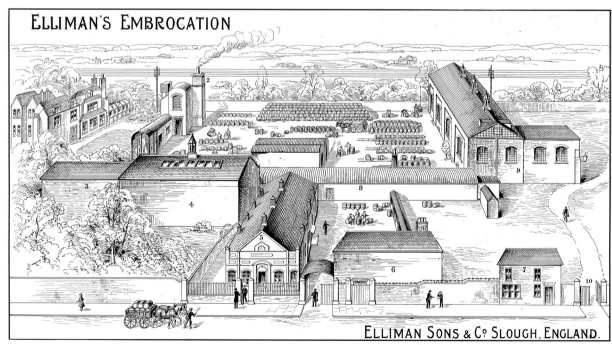

Key: **1**. Manager & South Entrance, **2**. Boiler, **3**. Stores, **4**. Machinery Hall, **5**. Offices, **6**. +. Stores, **8**. Filling Dept.,
9. Packing Dept., **10**. East Entrance. Storage for 2,500 casks of Embrocation in cellars **11**, **5**, **9**.

70.   James Elliman, Jnr, 1846-1924, was one of Slough's greatest benefactors. The Drill Hall, the fire station, the Public Hall and Salt Hill Park all benefited from his generosity.

71.   Elliman's Embrocation was widely advertised in posters, magazines, postcards and handbills. It was described as 'An Excellent Good thing'. The firm's shrewd grasp of the importance of advertising must have been at least partly responsible for the phenomenal worldwide success of the embrocation, which, at the height of its fame, was being exported to 42 countries.

I have a *notion* you must either pull him over or persuade him to pull you back again.

BRUMBY & CLARKE LTD HULL.

Elliman's for the Ankles and no mistake.

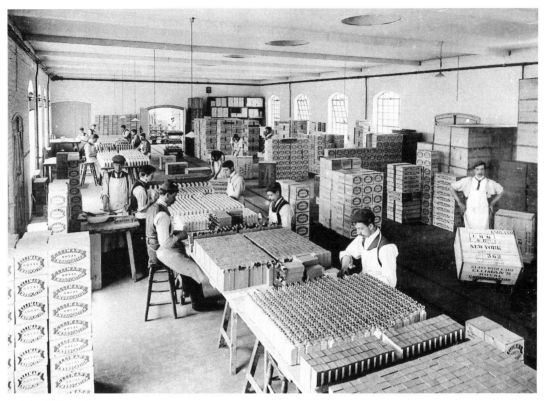

72.   Elliman's packing department in the Chandos Street factory, *c*.1895. To the right a man is about to load a crate destined for New York.

73.   The loading bay of Elliman's factory, *c*.1895. The transport is, appropriately, horse-power – Elliman's Royal Embrocation (shown in the photograph) was made specifically for use on animals, particularly horses. Universal Embrocation was for human use.

74. The Horlicks factory tower is clearly seen from trains travelling through Slough and for many years was one of the town's most distinctive pieces of architecture. The factory was built in 1906 and production of Horlicks malted milk started there in 1908.

75. During the First World War the War Office bought part of Cippenham Court Farm, just west of Farnham Road, to turn into a motor vehicle repair depot. This photograph shows the foundations of one of the first service buildings on the site being dug. So eager were the authorities to begin the task that, at a time of severe nationwide food shortages, they did not even bother to harvest the standing crop.

76.   Aerial photograph of Timbertown, which was situated off the Farnham Road on a site now occupied by the Sir William Herschel Grammar School. Timbertown was an estate of single-storey homes built, as the name suggests, of wood. Only ever intended as temporary accommodation for workers at the depot, Timbertown was demolished during the 1930s.

77.   From the outside the Timbertown houses looked rather like army barracks, but inside they were spacious and comfortable.

78.   When the war ended in 1918 the Slough Motor Vehicle Depot, or 'Dump' as it had been nicknamed, became obsolete and a financial embarrassment to the government. However, it was bought by a group of businessmen who intended to repair and sell the broken cars, lorries and motor cycles and in 1920 the Slough Trading Company was born. Even before the last of the vehicles had been sold, some of the buildings no longer needed were rented out as factories – a pioneer idea in 1920. In 1926 the trading company became Slough Estates Ltd.

79.   The main entrance to Slough Trading Estate during the 1930s. The Trading Estate was for some years almost like a town within a town, with its own gates, boundaries, post office, banks, power station, railway station and fire and ambulance crews.

80. One of the reasons for the choice of Slough as the location for the War Office Motor Repair Depot was the proximity of the site to the main Great Western Railway line from London to the West. For several years the Trading Estate had its own branch lines which joined up with the main line, giving the factories excellent transport links. It even had its own station for the use of workers, as shown in this photograph. After the Second World War use of the railway gradually diminished. The last passenger train ran in 1956 and the very last train to use the line ran in April 1973.

81. The cooling towers on the Trading Estate have been a landmark since they were built in the 1920s.

82. Many of the factories along the Bath Road displayed façades in the Art Deco style which was fashionable in the late 1920s and '30s, though the walls not facing the road were usually built in a very functional style.

83.   The Modern Wheel Drive (originally called the Four Wheel Drive) was the second firm to lease a factory on the Estate. The English branch of the American Company was founded for the purpose of taking over lorries from the Disposal Board and rebuilding them. It also had a licence for manufacturing new four wheel drive lorries.

84. A group of workers outside Vitatex & Co. factory, *c.*1934. Vitatex manufactured good quality underwear.

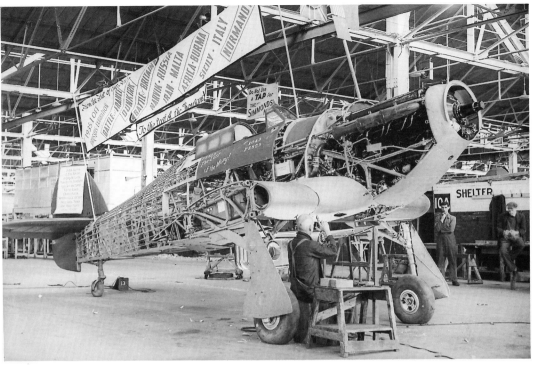

85. In 1936 the Hawker Aircraft factory was established in Langley. The firm's chief designer was Sydney Camm who built his first aeroplane when he lived in Windsor. He designed the Hurricane fighter plane seen here being assembled. At the peak of production in 1942 five Hurricanes were completed each day. The factory also built other planes, but by 1950 its grass airfield was no longer adequate and the firm left the area, leasing much of the site to the Ford Motor Company.

86. An impressive display of Tempest II aeroplanes lined up by the side of the runway at Hawker's factory at Langley.

87. Lidstone's original High Street premises photographed in the 1930s. The bakery firm was founded by William Albert Lidstone who took over Lovegrove's old bakery business in 1880. His son, Gilbert, can be seen between the two horses.

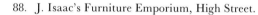

88. J. Isaac's Furniture Emporium, High Street.

89. Colgate's, in Alpha Street, purveyors to Eton College; it was replaced by a shop in the High Street.

90. The original Co-op shop in Slough High Street, in the 1890s. The Slough and District Co-operative Society was formed in 1892 as a way of relieving the distressed families of brickmakers who were striking for higher wages.

91. The Cippenham branch of the Co-op began in a wooden hut which had been used as a canteen by the War Depot. The Co-op took over when the Depot closed and erected a new hut in 1920, large enough to feed 240 workers at a sitting. It later became a shop until it was replaced by a new purpose-built store at Everitts Corner in 1930. This building was only recently demolished. Turnover in 1929 was £3,198 16s. 9d.

92. Opening a new branch of the Co-op in Manor Park Estate.

Buildings & Services

93.   The new parish church at Slough, known since 1851 as St Mary's, was consecrated on 1 July 1837. The original building, the left half of the church in the photograph, was criticised as ugly and small. In 1876 the foundation stone of a more elaborate extension, the right half of the church in the photograph, was laid.

94.   St Laurence's Church, Upton. This was the original parish church of Upton cum Chalvey in which for centuries Slough was only a small village. By the 1820s it had become too small for the growing population and was virtually abandoned after St Mary's was built. However, after a period of neglect when sheep were allowed to graze at will, it was restored and re-consecrated in 1851.

95. Upton Court was built in the mid-14th century as a manor house for Upton Manor. During the 600 years it has been occupied there have been many alterations to the main building, but none more drastic than the restoration taking place today. This photograph was taken in the 1930s.

96. The dining table at Upton Court set for a sumptuous Christmas dinner during the 1930s. The maid who had laid the table was, understandably, very proud of her handiwork.

97. Observatory House in Windsor Road, Slough, was the home of the astronomer Sir William Herschel from 1786 to his death in 1822. The house was home to his sister, Caroline, a distinguished astronomer in her own right, and his wife, Lady Herschel, and his son, Sir John Herschel, who was to become an important physicist. He was also president of Slough Mechanics' Institute, the forerunner of the Leopold Institute.

98. The circular flower bed in the garden behind Observatory House marked the location of the base of Herschel's most ambitious telescope, 40 ft. long and built entirely to his own design and specification. Herschel's discovery in 1781, while living in Bath, of the planet Uranus doubled the known size of the universe. His own words, written in 1784, are perhaps his best epitaph: 'I have looked further into space than any human being before me. I have seen stars whose light, it will be proved, has taken two million years to reach us.'

99. The *Crown* was one of the most important inns in the 18th and 19th centuries when Slough was a village and stage on the Bath Road. The sign in the photograph claims that the inn was established in 1315, but the first documentary reference is a licence issued in 1618.

100. The new 'Old' *Crown Inn* was built in 1933 on the site of the old hotel by the Courage Brewery as part of their policy of improvement. The building has since been demolished, but the name, Crown Corner, lingers on.

101.   The original railway station at Slough was opened in 1840, two years after the railway line was completed. The delay was caused by opposition from the authorities at Eton College who objected to the building of a station so close to Eton in case it encouraged boys to abscond to London! The large building to the right was the original *Royal Hotel*, owned by the Great Western Railway. The young Queen Victoria and Prince Albert regularly used Slough station and had their own waiting room within the hotel. However, when the Slough to Windsor branch line was built the hotel lost so much business that it became uneconomical and was closed in 1853.

102.   An alternative station (designed by Brunel) was built at Langley, but when the Great Western Railway Company was persuaded to allow trains to stop at Slough without the benefit of platforms or stations, the Langley station remained unused. Despite petitions from the people of Langley and neighbouring villages, the station did not open for eight years.

EXECUTION

OF JOHN TAWELL,

AND FULL CONFESSION, TO HIS WIFE, IN A LETTER

Of the Murder of Sarah Hart.

Aylesbury,
This morning, 8 o'clock.

At an early hour this morning, the sheriffs, with their usual attendants, arrived at the prison, and after partaking of some refreshment, proceeded to the condemned cell, where they found the reverend ordinary engaged in prayer with the wretched culprit.

After the usual formalities had been observed of demanding the delivery of the body of the prisoner into their custody, Tawell was conducted to the press-room, where his irons were struck off. The executioner, with his assistants, then commenced pinioning his arms, which operation they skilfully and quickly despatched. During these awful preparations he sighed deeply, but uttered not a word. At a quarter before 8, all the arrangements having been completed, the bell of the prison commenced tolling, and the melancholy procession was formed:— the reverend ordinary, preceding the culprit on his way to the fatal drop, began reading in a distinct tone, the burial service for the dead. No sound, if we except the deep sighs of the unhappy man, interrupted the clergyman, as the procession moved along the subterranean passage. On arriving at the steps leading to the scaffold, he turned round, and tremulously thanked the sheriffs and the worthy governor of the prison, for their kind attentions to him during his confinement. Then, firmly but with a slow motion, he ascended the scaffold, on reaching which he was placed in the necessary position. Whilst the executioner was adjusting the fatal apparatus of death, which was done in an incredibly short space of time, Tawell was deeply absorbed in prayer. The executioner, having drawn the cap over his face, retired from the scaffold; and, on the signal being given, the bolt was withdrawn, and the unhappy man was launched into eternity. A few convulsive struggles were perceptible, and he ceased to exist. After hanging the usual time, the body was cut down, and conveyed into the prison.

Wednesday, March 12.

At 10 o'clock the judges took their seats upon the bench, at the Court-house, Aylesbury; and shortly afterwards the prisoner was brought in. The indictment having been read, accusing John Tawell with the murder of Sarah Hart, the counsel for the prosecution opened the case, and called the following witnesses.

Mary Anne Ashley—I live in Bath Place, Salt Hill. On the 1st of January I saw the prisoner enter deceased's house, which was next door to mine; and between six and seven in the evening I heard a stifled

sort of scream, and saw the prisoner coming out of Mrs. Hart's house. I said, I am afraid my neighbour is ill; but the prisoner, who appeared agitated, made no reply. When I got inside her door, deceased was lying on the floor, with her petticoats nearly up to her knees, and the left stocking was down and a bun. I found nothing deleterious tory, and her left shoe off: her cap was a little distance from her: she was making a noise, and her eyes were fixed. I spoke to her, but she made no reply. Froth came from the corners of her mouth, and she appeared to be dying. I went to the landlady's, (Mrs. Wheeler's), the last house in the row, and Mrs. Barrett, a relative of Mrs. Wheeler's, returned with me. We placed a pillow on the child's chair and put deceased's head upon it, and sent for Dr. Champneys. On Mrs. Hart's table, when I first went in, there was a bottle, and a glass with some porter, and another glass with only a little froth in it. Deceased spoke, previously to the scream, in rather a loud tone, but only a few words.

Mr. J. Cooper—I am a practical chemist, and was formerly lecturer on chemical jurisprudence. Mr. Champneys and two other gentlemen called on me and requested me to test the contents of a human stomach, which they produced a bottle, another bottle with some porter, some porter in a glass, and a bun. I found nothing deleterious either in the porter or the bun; but I found proofs of the presence of prussic acid in the contents of deceased's stomach. In the bottle there must have been about a grain of pure prussic acid. Cross-examined —As to the effect of prussic acid on the stomach, I have no experience, but judge only by analogy service at Streatham Hill, Surrey. I went to deceased's house, where I saw the prisoner for possessing a forged Bank of England note, where his good conduct obtained for him emancipation. Knowing something of chemistry, he soon amassed a considerable sum in that line, and entered into several trading trans-

ill, and vomitted about a handful blame on the stout. The jury returned a verdict of guilty, and the judge pronounced sentence of death upon him.

Copy of a Letter from the Prisoner to his Wife.

"My dear Wife,
"I pray thee to forgive the injury I have done thee. If thou art not, to whom shall I look? Oh! pray for me, my dear, dear wife. When thy soul shall be inspired by the Holy Spirit, let thy wretched husband's misery cause thee to pray for him. That I did commit the horrid crime I now confess, and I also made the attempt last September. I am, dear wife, your wretched husband

"JOHN TAWELL."

He was transported to Sydney for possessing a forged Bank of England note, where his good conduct obtained for him emancipation. Knowing something of chemistry, he soon amassed a considerable sum in that line, and entered into several trading trans-

actions. After living 15 years in Sydney, he returned home, where he has been endeavouring to gain admittance as a member of the Society of Friends, to which body he belonged before his transportation, but they would not admit him. During his first wife's illness, the deceased nursed her, whence arose their illicit correspondence.

COPY OF VERSES.

GOOD people all of each degree
Attend to what I shall unfold.
It is a dreadful tragedy
Will make your very blood run cold.
Your hearts alas with grief will bleed,
When you this cruel tale shall hear;
There's not been done so vile a deed
Since the days of Courvoisier.

John Tawell is my name, 'Tis true,
In wealth and splendour once I've dwelt,
A hypocrite I've always been,
Nor meek eye upon her never felt.
My first crime was Forgery,
A convict was to Sidney sent,
I riches gain'd oh! misery,
My stubborn heart did not relent.

To lustful passions I gave way,
At virtue I had always smiled.
Poor Sarah Hart I did betray,
She by me had proved with child,
My house she left, yet still the same,
In adulterous love we pass'd our time,
In unholy deeds of guilt and shame:
My wife unconscious of our crime.

Two smiling babes by me she bore,
Oh! what a wretch thus to betray
Her from the paths of virtue tore.
And then to take her life away!
To Salt-hill in Buckinghamshire,
Poor Sarah Hart, she did remove,
There I to her did oft repair,
To carry on our guilty love.

Grown tired at last, yet full of grief,
Oh God! poor thing, I did her slay,
With prussic acid poison vile,
I took her harmless life away.
While she her glass had pledg'd to me
And drank my health for many a year,
Oh! what a monster I must be,
With poison I had drugged her beer.

Cut off in life, sent to the tomb,
With all her sins upon her head,
Would I could recall her doom,
And raise her once more from the dead,
For none had seen my victim fall,
For some to save or help was nigh,
Yet one above had witnessed all,
'Twas God's allseeing, piercing eye.

I was taken, tried and cast,
My gold in hundreds flew amain:
To save my life all hope is past,
My gold alas, was all in vain,
And I must die in ignominy,
For death in terror now I wait,
O shun that crime, adultery,
Take warning by a murderer's fate.

Next Friday I am doomed to die,
While gaping thousands round appear
None will heave a pitying sigh,
Nor for the murderer drop a tear.
Hark, hark! they come ! I hear their tread,
The executioner now I see,
I'll soon be number'd with the dead,
Great God of mercy pardon me.

Distant view of the cottage where the murder was committed, Bath Place, Salt Hill.

J. Paul & Co., Printers, (Successors to the late J. Catnach) 2 & 3, Monmouth-court, Seven Dials.

103. In 1846 John Tawell was convicted of the murder of Susan Hart, his mistress who lived at Salt Hill. He was the last man to be hanged from the upper window of the Court House at Aylesbury, and the first person to be caught for a crime through the use of the electric telegraph. The first Electric Magnetic Telegraph was installed at Paddington in 1839 and extended to Slough in 1843; the telegraph office was on a small hillock close to the railway.

104. Slough station was rebuilt in 1884, by which time the original station had become too small to support the needs of a fast growing town. When this photograph was taken in the early years of the 20th century Slough had an important service depot for the G.W.R.'s 'bus fleet'.

105. The new *Royal Hotel*. The stables and laundry of the old *Royal Hotel* were converted into a new hotel, less 'magnificent' than the old, but still a good class railway hotel. This advertisement appeared in the local newspaper in 1938.

106. The old *Royal Hotel* was sold and in 1863 it became the British Orphan Asylum which was opened in June of that year by the Prince and Princess of Wales, the future King Edward VII and Queen Alexandra, who travelled by train to Slough to be present. The picture shows ladies presenting purses of donations towards the cost of the asylum. After the opening ceremony the Prince and Princess each planted a tree in the grounds in commemoration of the events of the day.

107. The British Orphan Asylum at the turn of the century. In 1920 the building was taken over by the Licensed Victuallers' School; it was rebuilt in 1938. The new building was in turn demolished when the School left Slough in 1989.

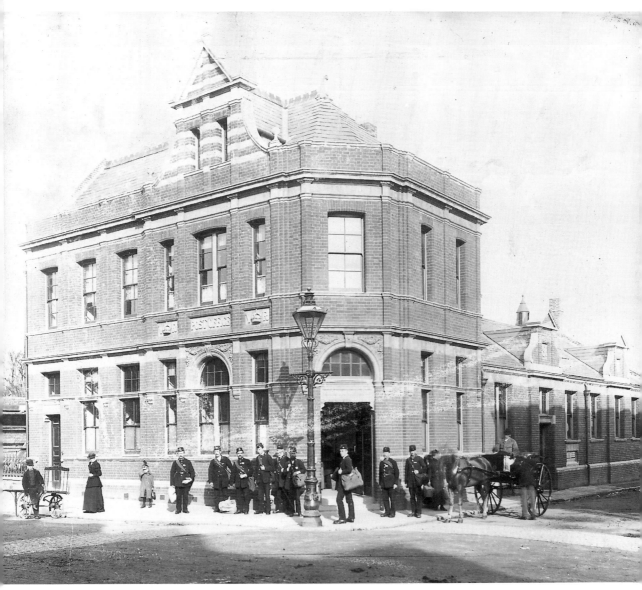

108. Slough's first postmistress, Maria Luff, was appointed in 1841 when Slough took over from Colnbrook as the postal town because the mail now travelled by rail. Her premises were in Buckingham Place. A purpose-built post office was erected in 1893 on the corner of Slough High Street and Chandos Street. It was demolished in 1973, a new General Post Office having opened just behind it in the new Queensmere shopping centre the year before.

109. The sorting office, *c.*1906. The room is lit by gas and the sorting of the mail was done by hand.

110. This photograph of Slough High Street, taken looking west at the turn of the century, gives a good view of the Slough Public Hall and Leopold Institute. The Institute was opened in 1887 and named after Queen Victoria's youngest son, Prince Leopold. James Elliman gave the land for the building. The building was demolished in 1972 as part of the Town Centre redevelopment; a new Public Hall was built in Herschel Street.

111. The Drill Hall stood at the corner of Wellington Street and Chandos Street. It was given by James Elliman in 1902 to provide accommodation for 'C' Company 1st Buckinghamshire Rifle Volunteer Corps. This was at the time of the Boer War in South Africa, in which the Volunteers fought. Part of the Queensmere shopping centre now stands on the site of the hall.

112. In 1897 James Elliman Jnr. built a fire station for Slough Volunteer Fire Brigade in Mackenzie Street. In 1921 the brigade acquired two new engines, Hannah and Mary, here seen proudly displayed outside the station. The station was recently demolished and replaced by a modern station near to the Three Tuns crossroads.

113. Botham's *Windmill Hotel* after the fire which destroyed it on the night of 21 April 1882. It had already been closed and sold for use as a school. The present *Windmill* public house was built by Wethered's Brewery on the site of the tap of the old hotel.

114. This is how the *Windmill Inn* had looked before it was destroyed by fire. The *Windmill* at Salt Hill was one of the best inns along the Bath Road. It was a stage coach inn in the mid-18th century, but by the early 19th century had become a high class posting house – only to lose much of its trade when the railway came to Slough.

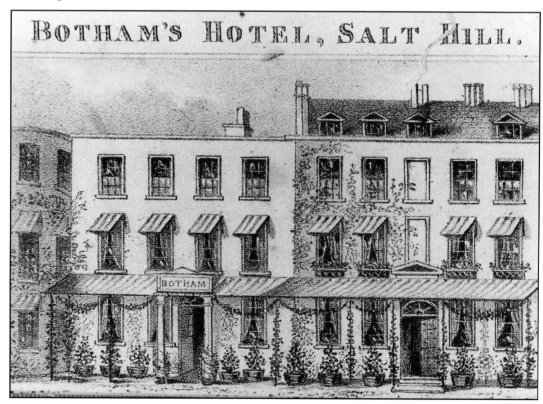

115. St Paul's parish was created in 1905 from parts of Upton cum Chalvey and Stoke Poges parishes because of the increased population of this part of Slough north of the railway line. When the church was opened in 1906 it lay on the edge of the built-up area. The Nash family gave the land and bricks from the family firm were used in building the church.

116. Dignitaries posing for a photograph at the opening of the Methodist Church on Ledgers Road in 1901.

117. Baylis House was built in about 1695 for Dean Hascard, a country gentleman. It was considerably enlarged in the early 18th century for Dr. Henry Godolphin, Provost of Eton College, when a third storey was added. From 1829 to 1907 it was a very good Roman Catholic School. After a fire in the 1950s, the original elevation was reconstructed in the restoration.

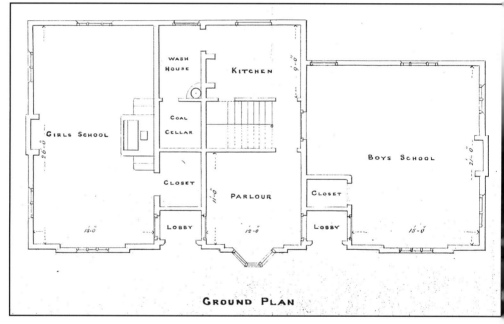

GROUND PLAN

ELEVATION

118a. & b. Plan of Upton National School, 1851. The school consisted of living accommodation for the schoolmaster and two large rooms, one for the boys of all ages, and the other for the girls. A few years later a third room was built to accommodate the infants.

119. Cippenham School adjoined the Mission Church on the Green. This early 20th-century photograph shows the headmistress outside talking to a young teacher from Burnham. Until very recently Cippenham was part of Burnham parish.

120. Children from Cippenham School at the turn of the century. The child in a dress with very short hair is a boy. It was not unusual for boys of poor families to wear their older sisters' dresses until there was a pair of trousers to fit them.

121. Slough National School, 1908. This was the successor of the Upton National School.

122.   Slough Secondary School for boys and girls was opened in January 1912. This illustration is taken from the 1911 prospectus; the school was the first state secondary school in the town.

123.   Halidon House School in Mackenzie Street was a well respected school for girls. This photograph of its science laboratory was probably taken in the 1930s. Note the chart showing the metric system of weights and measures, evidence of progressive attitudes.

124.   Class IV at the Tonman Mosley Junior School, Slough, *c.*1927. The teacher, thought to be Miss Pickard, had more than 40 pupils to care for – no wonder she is concentrating on the class and not looking at the camera. Tonman Mosley was a local politician and magistrate with a particular interest in education.

125. The Eton Union Workhouse on Albert Street was opened in 1836 in response to the Poor Law Amendment Act of two years earlier. Providing strictly segregated accommodation for the destitute of Slough and other parishes in the Union, it was a place that was dreaded, particularly by the old and infirm. It was the old people's home, doss house for tramps, home for unmarried mothers, infirmary for the sick poor, orphanage and lunatic asylum.

126. Slough Town Hall as it looked when it was opened in 1937. The old building remains virtually unchanged, but a large extension has been added to the rear and left, with a new main entrance off Ledgers Road.

127. Lydia Simmons, the first black lady mayor in Slough or anywhere else in the country – another first for Slough.

At Leisure

128. A group of Slough scouts at camp in 1910. The first troop of Boy Scouts was formed in Slough in 1908, only one year after Baden-Powell published his book on scouting for boys. The first Slough Company of Girl Guides followed in 1915.

129. A familiar sight in Slough during the 1920s and 1930s was the De Haviland Moth Biplane flown by Morris and Nigel Jackaman, two brothers whose family at that time owned the land on which the Town Hall is built. During the early years of aviation when aeroplanes were a rare sight and there were no formal air traffic control regulations, the two brothers often flew to the south coast for an early morning swim before breakfast.

130. The entrance to the Salt Hill Recreation Grounds on the corner of the Bath Road and Stoke Poges Lane. The park was created on land which had once belonged to the Godolphin family. Sadly, the magnificent iron eagles were melted down, along with the railings which surrounded the playing fields, during the Second World War. The park was given to the town by James Elliman and opened in 1907.

131. The Barn was built as the tea and refreshment rooms for Salt Hill Recreation Grounds. It is still there today in the middle of the park, clearly visible from the Bath Road.

132. For many years the park had a children's paddling pool at the back, close to the railway line.

133.   During the 1930s and 1940s several of the factories on the Trading Estate had their own sports teams. This is the St Helen's Company's team in 1947.

134.   The Cygnets hockey team, 1933-4. They played for the Light Production Company on Slough Trading Estate which made pistons and other parts for cars. The ladies embroidered their badge of a cygnet on their own tunics; the cygnet was the company's logo.

135. The Slough Social Centre was
one of the first of its kind in the
country. This photograph shows
Queen Mary arriving at the Centre on
26 April 1937, soon after it was
opened. In December of the same year
Their Majesties King George and
Queen Elizabeth visited the Centre.

136. The Centre aimed to provide
sport and recreational facilities for
workers on the Trading Estate and
other work places in Slough, although
membership was open to all. Many
firms paid part of the subscription for
their employees.

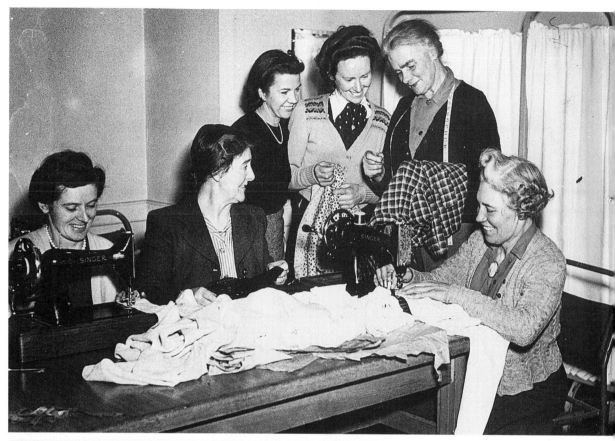

137. Ladies in a sewing class at the Centre in the 1940s.

138. The swimming pool was built when the Centre was opened and has been regularly used ever since.

139.   The Granada Cinema on the Windsor Road opened in
1938, shortly after the opening of the Social Centre. It had a
very elaborate interior, typical of the late 1930s. This
photograph was taken in 1949; the cinema was demolished
in 1987.

140.   The interior of the Adelphi Cinema on the Bath Road.
Opened in 1930, the Adelphi was a grand building,
containing a ballroom as well as a cinema. The building is
still standing and now hosts bingo – organised by Granada.

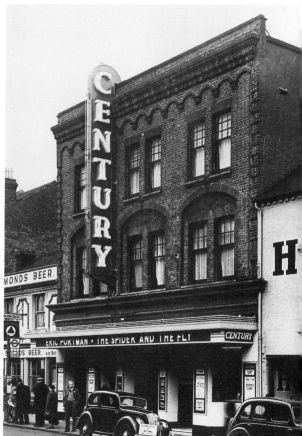

141. The Empire Cinema, Chalvey, in about 1912. This was not quite the first cinema in town; that honour went to the Slough Picture Hall which opened behind the *Crown* in 1910.

142. The Palace Cinema on Slough High Street opened in 1921. It was renamed the Century in 1949 and closed in 1957.

143. Times and values change. Black and white minstrel groups were not considered offensive many years ago, as this 1909 photograph of the flourishing Slough and Chalvey Black Diamond Minstrel Group bears witness.

144. (*right*) Slough Cricket Club match played at the *Dolphin* field in 1892. The club is reputed to have been in existence by 1850; it still plays today.

145. (*below*) The Cippenham Top Hat cricket team and band on Cippenham Green in the 1930s. The match between the Cippenham team and a team chosen by the President, Dr. Maxwell Summers, was an annual event. The top hats were obtained from Eton College.

146.   Miss Blanchett's dancing class, 1926-7.

147.   St Mary's parish outing in the 1930s. The vicar was the Rev. Haggar.

148.   Opening of the Montem swimming pool.

149.   A nativity play in St Andrew's Church at Cippenham in the late 1930s.

Celebrations & Special Events

150. Salt Hill, Montem celebrations, 1778. The Montem Mound, a man-made mound of uncertain origin, was used for some three hundred years by Eton College scholars as the focus of their Montem celebration – a kind of rag day when money was collected to send the head colleger to Cambridge. The salt given by the boys in exchange gave the village its name. This drawing, showing George III and Queen Charlotte at the Montem celebrations in 1778, depicts an impossibly large mound.

151. Taking the family photograph in Victorian times was a great event. This delightful picture, taken about 1900, is of the well-known Barrett family of solicitors and local government officials. The boy standing at the back is Herbert Leslie Crossthwaite Barrett and the gentleman next to him is Richard Henry Barrett.

152. Christenings, marriages and funerals were family events which, then as today, were often judged by the outward show. This funeral procession is almost certainly that of John Harding who died in 1925. The hearse appears to have stopped outside his shop, a poulterer's and fishmonger's in the High Street, as a sign of respect. The almost deserted street suggests that the other shops had been closed for the occasion. Notice the three-storey building at the rear; this was probably the dwelling house and the single storey had been built in front over the original garden area.

153. The wedding of W. J. Ellwood and J. M. Brion in 1896.

154. Like almost every other town in the country, Slough celebrated Queen Victoria's Diamond Jubilee by building elaborate arches. This one was in Mackenzie Street and the railway station can be seen through the arch.

155. Hospital procession in Slough High Street, 16 September 1907. The procession raised money for the Slough Nursing fund and the King Edward VII Hospital at Windsor which was built the year this photograph was taken. Notice Charles Luff's shop; this was the house that Maria Luff, the town's first postmistress, took over in 1841. Her son started the printing works and *Slough Observer*.

156. Parades were occasions for enjoyment but they were also vital for the collection of money before the creation of the welfare state. This photograph appears to show a Co-op carnival.

157. At most parades and carnivals prizes were given for the best individual floats; this one represented the fish department of the Co-op shop in Slough High Street.

158. Hundreds of children filled Salt Hill park on Empire Day, 1909, when this picture was taken – every one of them wearing a hat. The initials on the banner are those of the Buckinghamshire, Berkshire and Oxfordshire Christian Mission Fellowship; prizes were won by children and groups collecting money for overseas missionary work.

159. The election wagon of the Langley branch of the South Bucks Conservative and Unionist Association in action during the 1910 elections. At this date Slough was part of the South Buckinghamshire constituency. The candidate, Sir Alfred Cripps, was a celebrated barrister who gave up his legal career to enter Parliament. He won the seat from the sitting Liberal member with a majority of 2,556. In 1914 he was created a peer and the inhabitants of South Buckinghamshire had to go to the polls again.

160. Great Western Railway staff posing during the celebrations for the coronation of George V.

161. Hunger march: men from Wales taking a welcome break in Slough. The 1920s and early 1930s were years of depression with mass unemployment over much of the country, though Slough escaped comparatively lightly because of the new Trading Estate.

162a.   The Chalvey Stabmonk. The strange 'Stabmonk' ceremony grew up during the late 19th century following the death of a travelling organ-grinder's monkey. The 'wake' for the dead monkey (which had been stabbed) involved a mock funeral after which one member of the crowd was pushed into the Chalvey Brook. He was then declared the unofficial 'mayor' for the ensuing year. This plaster image is reputed to be a cast of the original monkey. However the whole ceremony may be much older than any records, a rationalisation of older ceremonies.

162b.   The Chalvey Stabmonk ceremony in the 1930s. Similar parades continued as late as the 1960s, money being collected for local charities.

163. Silver Jubilee procession of the Slough Boys Brigade, 1935.

164. Buglers sound the reveille to wake up the mayor on the morning of Slough's Charter celebration. Slough was elevated to borough status on 14 September 1938.

165. Presentation of the Borough Charter.

166. The mayor's procession leaving the Town Hall on Charter Day.

167. The arms granted to the new borough reflect several aspects of the town's history. The swan symbolises Buckinghamshire and holds in its beak a pink which, along with the two roses, represents the horticultural interests of the Borough. Above these are two brick-axes, emblematic of the brickmaking industry, and the symbol of Uranus relating to the discovery of the planet by Sir William Herschel. The supporters are Mercury, God of Commerce, and Vulcan, God of Industry. The motto means 'By Confidence and Strength'.

FIDUCIA ET VI

168. Happy citizens celebrating the granting of the charter.

169. Employees from McMichael's factory take a break from work to be photographed in a trench for an air raid shelter being built near the Wexham Road Bridge in the early years of the Second World War. Notice the one man and the one shovel.

170. During the Second World War all the factories on Slough Trading Estate contributed in some way to the war effort. In 1941 the Lord Mayor of London visited the Estate and is here being shown around High Duty Alloys Ltd. by the Mayor of Slough, Mr. Noel Mobbs, and Ian Ross. The lady working the machine is wearing one of the hats issued during the war to factory workers.

171. On Wednesday morning, 7 May 1941, the mayor Alderman A. E. Ward climbed the ladder to secure the fifth – and final – section of the 30 ft. model of a destroyer which represented Slough's donations towards the purchase of a destroyer. Since the beginning of War Weapons Week the town had collected over £500,000 (mainly as National Savings Certificates) and before the end of the week an amazing £1,001,623 was raised.

172.   Food parcels from America are part of the memories of many who experienced the food shortages of the Second World War. Here Doris Blunden, well known for her welfare work, is seen distributing tins of steak and kidney pudding and 'camp' pie to local residents.

173.   Wartime battle for fuel at the Granada Cinema.

174.   Aspro evacuees Christmas party.

175. Land girls with the Duchess of Kent at the opening of their hostel in Chalvey Park in 1941.

176. Signals Division of the 'C' Company, Buckinghamshire Home Guards in their headquarters at Baylis House.

177. The people of the Wexham Road area of Slough celebrated V.E. Day in their own community centre, its lights brightening up the street after years of blackouts.

178. Street party in Salt Hill Way celebrating the end of the Second World War.

179. The Queen visits Slough during the Coronation celebrations in 1953.